THE FUNDAMENTALS OF MARRIAGE

HOWARD & DANIELLE TAYLOR
FOUNDERS OF MARRIAGE ON DECK

Marriage on Deck Publishing

The Fundamentals of Marriage: 8 Essential Practices of Successful Couples

Published in Los Angeles, California, by Marriage on Deck.

Marriage on Deck titles may be purchased in bulk for ministry, educational, business, fundraising, or sales promotional use. For information, please e-mail hello@marriageondeck.com.

Unless otherwise indicated, all Scripture quotations are taken from the Holy Bible, New International Version.

Other Scripture quotations are taken from the following: the Holy Bible, New Living Translation, copyright © 1996. Used by permission of Tyndale House Publishers Inc. Wheaton, Illinois 60189. All rights reserved.

Book Designer: Martina Daskalova

ISBN: 978-1-7346209-0-0

First printing edition, 2020

Printed in the United States of America

www.marriageondeck.com

TABLE OF CONTENTS

About the Authors

Howard and Danielle Taylor are entrepreneurs, marriage coaches, talk show hosts and the passionate creators behind Marriage on Deck; a marriage media ministry that has served over 4000 couples with its resources. They are passionate about inspiring couples to get married and stay married using biblical principles; and are frequent speakers at churches, conferences and seminars. Their show of the same name, showcases real couples addressing real issues facing marriages today and airs on the Christian Television Network.

Early on in their marriage, they had the dreadful position of sitting front row while the enemy chipped away at, broke down, and completely demolished several relationships amongst their close family and friends. After praying earnestly for those couples to emerge from the storm victoriously (some did, some didn't), they knew it was time to go on the offensive and get aggressive with the enemy. They begin to aggressively seek opportunities to educate couples and empower marriages through videos, seminars, conferences and now books. After going on a 7-day fast, Howard and Danielle felt commissioned by God to write a resource for couples to help identify and build on the 8 essential practices of successful couples.

It is their prayer that through the Fundamentals of Marriage Workbook, the wisdom of God, and the experiences they have been through, will help you and your spouse on your journey in this fraternity called marriage.

Howard & Danielle have been successfully married for 15 years and have birthed three sons; although one passed away at an early age. They have owned 7 businesses, their love language is traveling and they have visited over 20 countries.

COMMITMENT SHEET

Whether doing this with a group or just you and your spouse, there are a few guidelines that will ensure you have the best and most transformative experience. This commitment is intended to help set up a safe and helpful environment for you and anyone else you may be going through this workbook with. Take the time to read through it carefully together and sign the area below as a symbol of your commitment to this process, one another, and God.

I agree that:

1. I will do my best to approach this workbook with a positive attitude, as well as an open heart and mind to whatever God might do or reveal. (No workbook or amount of prayer can help you if you are closed off and your attitude stinks.)

2. I will focus on myself. All change starts with me. I cannot control anyone else's thoughts, beliefs, or actions. Thus, it is not helpful to focus on what they can do differently. (If you're elbowing your spouse about this point, you are already doing it wrong!)

3. I will go through this workbook with my spouse. I will have the necessary conversations with my spouse even when they are difficult, and I will put in the work required to set up my marriage for success. (You both have to be willing to do what is needed.)

4. I will not condemn, judge, or try to "fix" anyone that I go through this workbook with, including my spouse. Rather, I will love and respect others as I listen to and encourage them in their journey.

COMMITMENT SIGNATURE

I commit to the above guidelines in order to better my experience, the experience of my spouse, and the experience of any others I am going through this workbook with.

_____   _____

Signed   Date

INTRODUCTION
The Architect of Marriage

A lot of planning goes into the construction of a house. An architect works rigorously to make sure every measurement is set precisely so the house can stand strong and last for decades to come. It is then the construction foreman's responsibility to make sure those plans are carried out on the site. The foreman has to work closely with the architect to make sure the plans are fully understood.

When it comes to your marriage, you and your spouse are the foremen. You are both on-site making sure things are being built according to plan. The way your marriage is constructed is dependent on your guidance and understanding of what is supposed to take place. The question then becomes, whose plans are you using?

Perhaps you (knowingly or unknowingly) have modeled your marriage after your parents', assuming their way was the right way. Maybe you are engaged and have your own idea of what a spouse is supposed to be and what expectations they are to fulfill. It could be that you and your spouse are working from different blueprints and are in conflict regularly. And for some, you may simply float through marriage with no plan at all, defaulting to whatever seems good at the moment. No matter what your approach, it has become increasingly rare for a couple to ask themselves, "What is God's blueprint for our specific marriage?" and "Are we building our marriage accordingly?"

" I will guide you along the best pathway for your life. I will advise you and watch over you, says the Lord. - Psalm 32:8

Marriage is so integral to God's plan for his creation and he spares no time establishing instruction for the union in the very first chapter of the Bible. Why was it essential for God to establish his Fundamentals of Marriage for successful couples from Genesis to Revelation? Because marriage was created to be the governing entity over His creation. It is our belief that, when done in God's way, a single marriage positively impacts their family, which, in turn, positively impacts their neighborhood, which, in turn, positively impacts a community, which, in turn, positively impacts the world.

In the pages that follow, we will be exploring these *Fundamentals of Marriage* and the Architect that has put them in place. Whether you are newly engaged or have been married for years, God has a plan for your marriage and desires that you move forward in satisfaction and contentment. There will likely be difficult and uncomfortable conversations ahead. You may have to tear down old habits that have hindered you or negative thoughts that keep you from appreciating each other. But we assure you, nothing is too big for God and no marriage is beyond His repair. If you move forward with trust in God and show Christ-like love to one another, you will find that your marriage grows and thrives in a way you never dreamt possible.

> **❝ For the word of the Lord holds true, and everything he does is worthy of our trust. - Psalm 33:4**

It is our prayer that this workbook will serve you as a guide into these long-established truths and that your hearts will be open to Christ and what He desires for your marriage. Let's start building together.

How to Use This Workbook?

This workbook is made up of eight chapters that explore in detail various topics that are fundamental to your marriage. In each chapter, there are seven sections that will help you to engage with the focus of that chapter. The seven sections are as follows: (1) you will start by **Reading** together about that chapter's topic. (2) Then, you will take a moment of **Personal Reflection** with God to unpack what stood out to you in the reading. (3) Next, you will talk through **Discussion Questions** that really help you to engage with the topic. (4) After your discussion, you will each get to hear our personal perspectives on the chapter's focus in the **His Perspective** and (5) **Her Perspective** sections. (6) Finally, you will wrap up your time by reading and discussing a **Case Study** and (7) making note of the **Life Application** challenge at the end of each chapter. As you conclude each chapter, we recommend closing your time in prayer.

1

YOU AND I, WHY?

Finding Your Purpose

INTRO

Why did you get married? That is the million-dollar question most of us don't consider or talk about when we're contemplating walking down the aisle. As a matter of fact, we (Danielle and Howard) didn't discover why we got married or our purpose in marriage until we made a conscious decision (years after the wedding) to seek out why God brought us together in the first place. We've talked to many couples over the years and far too often couples float through their marriage with no goal or purpose in mind.

As you can see in the chart on the next page, a study of 1,306 couples revealed that 93% of married couples say they marry for love; 87% to have a lifelong commitment; 81% for companionship; 59% for children, and 31% say they married for financial stability. Although these are good reasons to marry, it's important to consider God's reason for your marriage. God has assigned each marriage a specific purpose so you can experience the joy and fulfillment God has always intended. So what is your God-given purpose together? In order to uncover this, we need to go back to when God first created marriage.

Why Get Married?

Percent of the general public saying _____ is a very important reason to get married.

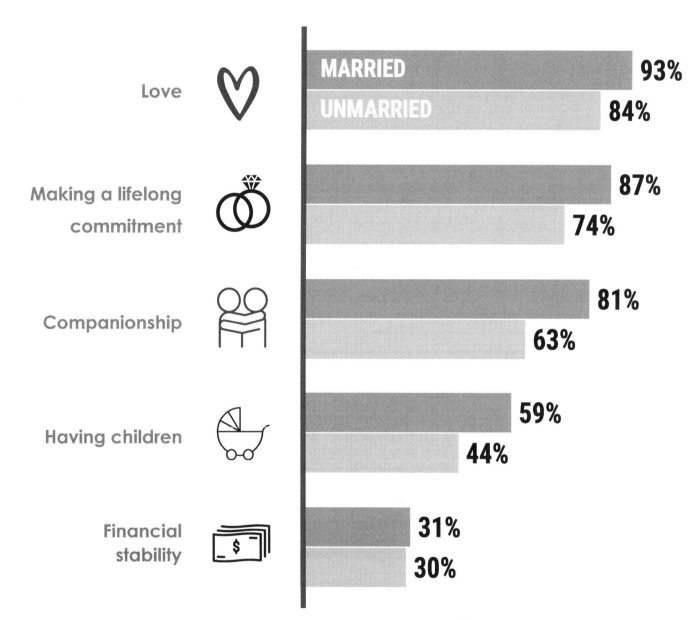

	MARRIED	UNMARRIED
Love	93%	84%
Making a lifelong commitment	87%	74%
Companionship	81%	63%
Having children	59%	44%
Financial stability	31%	30%

Source: Survey conducted May 10-13, 2013 (online poll)
Asked of married and unmarried separately, n=1,306 for married and 1,385 for unmarried.
Pew Research Center

In the Image of God

God created man and woman in His own image and considered us to be "very good." He then spoke 3 specific blessings over us, saying:

1. Be fruitful and increase in number;
2. Fill the earth and subdue it;
3. Rule over the fish in the sea and the birds in the sky and over every living creature that moves on the ground.[1]

Since we are made in His image, does that mean we will be perfect in marriage? No, but as His image-bearers, we are given purpose to rule as He rules, subdue the chaos as He did, play a part in the creation of life in His likeness, and have nothing rule over us except our good creator God. So how do we do this?

When reading this, most of us think God is simply telling us to have children. Though this is absolutely part of what God had in mind, we can't help but think about couples that cannot or have decided not to have children. Are they excluded from this part of God's charge? Of course not!

Be Fruitful

The word fruitful also means to be productive, helpful, beneficial, successful, useful, and the like. In order to be truly productive, we need to identify what gifts and talents God has given each of us as individuals and as a couple; asking how we might be useful with them in a way that honors Him and unites us in marriage.

---

[1] So God created mankind in his own image, in the image of God he created them; male and female he created them. God blessed them and said to them, "Be fruitful and increase in number; fill the earth and subdue it. Rule over the fish in the sea and the birds in the sky and over every living creature that moves on the ground... God saw all that he had made, and it was very good. And there was evening, and there was morning - the sixth day. Genesis 1:27, 28, 31

Multiply & Fill the Earth

It is expected that you reproduce yourself and God's Kingdom here on earth. Whether it is through your kids, friends, or anyone you may influence, God desires that you as a couple imprint on others the truth of who God is, of who they are (His image-bearers), and what that means for their lives. The charge then is not to simply bear children, but to fill the earth with those who would do what is right, love mercy, and walk humbly with their God.[2] It is not only important to understand your gifts but also how God is calling you to use them to bless those around you. Every couple is unique and we all need each other in God's Kingdom. Like a plant, we need to water the marriage God gave us so that we can grow, overflow, and be able to share what we have been given with others.

Subdue and Rule

Every marriage has been called to address and fix problems within your sphere of influence. One way to figure out what God is calling you to take control of is to ask, "what is/once was out of control in or around our marriage?" It could be your anger, your kids, your finances, your job, or an issue in the world around you.

Whatever your testimony is, use it to positively impact the community around you. The best story you can share with someone that may be struggling in life or marriage is your story. We are called to rule all things with the same goodness, grace, and justice that Jesus rules with.

---

[2] *He has shown you, O mortal, what is good. And what does the Lord require of you? To act justly and to love mercy and to walk humbly with your God. Micah 6:8*

Marriage How God Sees It

Sadly, throughout history, we have strayed far from God's original purpose. As a result, chaos and death gained dominion; and our earth was filled with murder, rape, incest, adultery, idolatry, war, and all sorts of evil. It is only by the power of Jesus that our world can be restored to the state God originally desired and our marriages are the vehicle that he chooses to do it through. By taking up our authority, subduing the chaos in this world, fruitfully living out our purpose, and multiplying our efforts through others, we work towards this purpose of having the marriage God intended for us to have.

PERSONAL REFLECTION

Take a few moments with yourself and God to write down the answer to the following question:

- Where do you feel out of control in your life and marriage? How would you like to see Jesus take back authority in your marriage?

DISCUSSION QUESTIONS

Take some time to discuss the following questions as a couple or group:

- What are your gifts and talents individually? How can you marry your gifts as a couple to work towards a common goal?

- How does this world seem to approach the purpose of marriage? What implications have you seen grow from this approach?

- How is pursuing purpose difficult when you do not understand your authority? Based on the passage from Genesis discussed in the reading, what authority has God given each of us as humans?

- Considering what you have read above, how would you like to see your marriage take on a new purpose; and what steps can you personally take to instill that purpose in your marriage?

HIS PERSPECTIVE

Marrying Danielle on July 30th, 2005, was the most joy-filled moment of my life, exceeding every momentous occasion to date. Why? I knew without a doubt that I was marrying my best friend. What was evident from our 4-year courtship was that good times were ahead of us. What was not as clear as the who (Danielle), was the what, when, where, and why. Like many couples, the simple magnitude of saying "I DO", had a profound impact on how we viewed a future that included tickets for two, not one. No longer was being an individualistic striver enough, as it didn't particularly draw us closer together. We desired a purpose that was shared between the two of us and we found our answer through prayer, fasting, and reading God's Word.

God revealed to us that he intended for our relationship to be a relatable witness to the world of his relationship and love for us. Additionally, and more specifically, we were to advocate and teach marriages about the time-proven marriage practices and principles revealed throughout the Bible. True marriage fulfillment comes from understanding that God created the gift of holy matrimony to enhance our ability to impact this world through combining our gifts and talents.

HER PERSPECTIVE

Learning the specific purpose for our marriage helped me to finally understand the unique role God had given Howard and I as a couple. The revelation gave me validation that there was more to our marriage than just doing life together and enjoying it in the process. It gave me an identity I didn't know I was seeking. I had a better idea of where we were going, what we were supposed to be doing, who we were called to impact, and how to focus our time and energy. Knowing our purpose also helped dictate what we were and weren't going to do, places we chose to go, and people we chose to spend time with, because life became all about fulfilling the purpose God had revealed to us in this season of our marriage. But how did we get here?

One December we went on a 7-day fast and committed to getting up every morning to pray together at 3 am. We prayed and asked God to show us how he wanted to use our marriage for the following year. Prior to this, we had been seeking God for career promotions and working on our businesses. Nothing is wrong with promotions or business; however, it becomes a problem when it is apart from or when it prevents us from being obedient to God. So during the fast, God gave us a clear answer! And believe it or not, the answer turned out to be what we had been doing all along, marriage ministry & business. But without recognizing it as our calling and purpose, we never would have approached it with the same sort of intentionality.

CASE STUDY

Greg and Christine met at a company picnic where they instantly hit it off and started spending all of their free time together. They would help each other on work projects, eat lunch together every day, and golf every Saturday without fail. They were truly each other's best friends. After about a year of dating, they got married in front of 100 of their closest family, friends, and co-workers. They continued to enjoy each other's company, attend golf tournaments, and explore different things they had in common. Although they attended church, Christine was more active in ministry than Greg; which didn't bother Christine because she knew that Greg was busy working on various projects at work and needing to bring work home.

However, once his busy season at work passed, Greg didn't bother to volunteer to serve at their church because he wasn't sure where his skills and interests would fit best. This became a source of contention in their marriage because Christine felt like Greg wasn't using his gifts and talents to serve the ministry as she had been. A few months later, Christine found out she was pregnant. Both her, Greg, their family, and friends were ecstatic. However, after only 6 months, Christine lost the baby. As Christine withdrew from ministry, Greg felt like this loss put a tug on his heart to serve other couples experiencing the same type of loss. After allowing adequate time to pass and much prayer, Greg and Christine thought it best to serve grieving families together.

Discuss with your spouse (or group) the takeaways from this case study. What went well, what went wrong? How did Greg and Christine find an opportunity to serve that touched both of their hearts and utilized their testimony?

LIFE APPLICATION

Spend some time praying about and brainstorming how you can be *fruitful, multiply, subdue,* and *rule* as a couple. Consider potential areas of passion, gifting,and calling that you both share and that would bring God glory. Write the first draft of a purpose statement for your marriage.

Be Fruitful:

_____

_____

_____

Multiply:

_____

_____

_____

Subdue and Rule:

_____

_____

_____

Our Purpose as a couple is...

_____

_____

_____

Reflections:

2

SECRET STABILITY:
Establishing a Strong Foundation

INTRO

Years ago, we planned a vacation to the beautiful city of Dubai. We saw all the advertisements of the rich and famous talking about how it was the place to visit. Since we love to travel, we saved up our money and set out on our trip, excited like two kids in a candy store for what we were about to see. For fun's sake, we dragged our two cousins along with us; getting them pumped up for months about all of the amazing places we were going to go, the food we would eat, the tours we planned to take, as well as the chance to see the tallest building in the world, the Burj Khalifa. Tourists from all over the world marvel at the 2,700-foot skyscraper as it seems to climb endlessly into the clouds above the city... and we were no exception.

But the foundation of the Burj Khalifa, hidden deep below the desert sand, is actually just as incredible as the building itself. Through research, we learned that the building is built on top of more than 5 million cubic feet of concrete weighing a remarkable 220 million pounds! Though this massive anchor is rarely thought of, this incredible super-structure would undoubtedly topple over without it.

This principle can be applied to our marriages as well. Some of us have met couples that are like skyscrapers. They have been married for forty, fifty, or even sixty years and genuinely seem to still be in love and content with each other. These marriages deserve to be admired and marveled at. Their testimonies are immense and beautiful. We often try to reproduce or emulate the external success, but rarely do we ask of these relationships, "what is the hidden foundation that allows this marriage to make it this far?"

The strongest foundation for any area of our lives is in Jesus and His teaching. He gives us the core values and principles on which our marriage should be built. As the Architect of marriage, God establishes that He is the center point, strong foundation, and most important ingredient to a healthy marriage. Because of this, a healthy marriage requires that God truly comes first.

> ❝ Therefore everyone who hears these words of mine and puts them into practice is like a wise man who built his house on the rock. - Matthew 7:24

Relationship With God

Putting God first and setting Him up as your foundation starts with relationship. Just like the foreman and the architect, your relationship with God is of vital importance to building a healthy marriage. Through faith in Jesus, God offers all of us this relationship and it grows with a regular diet of prayer and reading of the Scripture. To some this may seem overly basic, but when we ask couples if they regularly read God's Word and pray together, they rarely respond with a "Yes." Both of these practices help immensely toward bending our focus and hearts toward what God has for our marriage.

Learning God's Voice

The Bible is God's written word that He uses to teach, challenge, encourage, and personally speak to us. Reading the Bible is also the best way for us to learn who God is and what His voice sounds like. The more we read it, the more we will be able to recognize the unique timbre and tone of God's voice and gain the wisdom of His plan for our marriage. You will even realize that God can speak words of encouragement to your spouse through you and the scriptures you have stored in your heart. By reading it on your own and as a couple, it will help you both to better know His heart and can love each other better as a result. Sometimes we're too busy or feel like the Bible is too boring to read and study. However, if you don't know what God says about being a wife or a husband, how to raise your kids, or handle conflict, then how will you know the best action to take?

Connecting with God

Prayer, put simply, is intentionally connecting with God. As with anyone else, this connection comes through talking to, listening to, and simply sitting with Him. You can easily introduce this relational connection with God into your marriage by connecting with God on behalf of and with your spouse. Though sometimes prayer can seem intimidating, the Bible teaches that because of Jesus' sacrifice for us, we can approach God as His deeply beloved children.[3] When we pray, we can be honest with God about where we are, knowing that he will love us no matter what. Jesus also says that prayer isn't about putting on a show or saying the right words. When we pray, we can speak as we would to a trusted friend or family member, with no feeling of needing to impress Him.

These two components are indispensable when it comes to developing a healthy relationship with God and each other.

> 66 And when you pray, do not be like the hypocrites, for they love to pray standing in the synagogues and on the street corners to be seen by others. Truly I tell you, they have received their reward in full. But when you pray, go into your room, close the door and pray to your Father, who is unseen. Then your Father, who sees what is done in secret, will reward you. And when you pray, do not keep on babbling like pagans, for they think they will be heard because of their many words. Do not be like them, for your Father knows what you need before you ask him - Matthew 6:5-8

---

[3] But to all who believed him and accepted him, he gave the right to become children of God. John 1:12

PERSONAL REFLECTION

Take a few moments with yourself and God to write down the answer to the following question:

- What foundation do I currently trust in for my marriage? What do I hope holds my marriage up when things get difficult?

_____

_____

_____

_____

_____

- Do I have unrealistic expectations for myself or my spouse when it comes to marriage?

_____

_____

_____

_____

_____

DISCUSSION QUESTIONS

Take some time to discuss the following questions as a couple or group:

- How much time do you think most couples spend building a strong foundation in their marriage?

_____

_____

- Where have you seen examples of strong foundations and examples of weak foundations?

_____

_____

- How do you think prayer and reading the scripture can be helpful to building a strong foundation for your marriage? How can they help you align with God's plan?

_____

_____

- What do you do now to regularly strengthen your marriage? How is your marriage impacted by this practice (or lack thereof)?

_____

_____

HIS PERSPECTIVE

When grief unexpectedly struck our home through the loss of our first child (he passed away after only 4 days), Danielle and I were experiencing one of the most turbulent times of our marriage. During this season, our marriage could have toppled had it not been for the firm foundation we established during the formative years of our relationship. As the storm of emotions beat against the walls of our marriage physically, mentally, and spiritually, we retreated to our safe space of honesty and transparency, not judgment and criticizing. Because we grew comfortable praying with each other prior to the storm, we created a stronger bond after our mourning subsided. We also established a "no break-up to make up policy" in the early years of dating, training us to not seek physical separation or divorce as a readily available option in response to life's trying times.

HER PERSPECTIVE

When Howard and I first started dating, we made it a point to regularly read our Bible and pray together every night. Granted, we were only 18 and 19 years old with nothing but time on our hands, but I had no idea how impactful this would be on not only our dating relationship, but also our marriage that was to come. It helped us to establish a healthy foundation focused on Christ and what he wanted for us.

Although no marriage is perfect and we've certainly had our losses (failed business and the loss of our son) I attribute 100% of our marital successes, our friendship, and our overall happiness with each other to the foundation we built in Christ and continue to fortify. It really allowed us to see each other as God saw us and to learn how to treat each other with love, grace, and respect. It wasn't always easy, but we're still striving towards keeping our foundation grounded and firm in Christ every day.

CASE STUDY

Carlos and Janine were introduced to each other by a mutual friend. As with any new dating relationship, the butterflies and excitement were at an all-time high; so they felt they were making the best decision when after only three weeks of knowing each other, they got married. Plus, Carlos was a successful, widowed dad of five and always dreamed about the day he would find companionship and be able to give his children a mother figure. Janine, on the other hand, didn't have any children of her own and was excited at the prospect of becoming a step-mom. In addition, a few months before she met Carlos, she quit her job to start an art studio, a life-long dream of hers. Even though art was her passion and she couldn't imagine doing anything different, she was struggling to make ends meet. Therefore, meeting and marrying Carlos, a successful, seemingly nice, widowed father, made perfect sense. It seemed like a benefit for all.

However, it wasn't long into their new marriage that the reality of not really getting to know each other started to put a strain on their relationship. Carlos and Janine would bicker and fight over everything. They could hardly agree on anything and had differing perspectives as to how the kids should be raised. Their sex life was non-existent, and they were both miserable. Finally, Carlos recommended they go see a counselor to help them improve their communication and understanding of each other's needs. The first question the counselor asked them was why they got married so quickly. Neither said anything. They didn't want to hurt each other. In reality, though, Carlos only married Janine because she was attractive and he was lonely. And Janine only married Carlos because he was attracted to her and had enough financial stability to sustain both of them. After asking a series of questions, it became apparent that the struggles Carlos and Janine were having were not only due to not really knowing each other, but also for not aligning their goals, values, and interests as a couple. They had no common vision to fall back on and no foundation to support them. So when things got tough, it felt easier to just throw in the towel.

Discuss with your spouse (or your group) the takeaways from this case study. What went well, what went wrong? How could a healthy foundation have helped Carlos and Janine? How can they move forward now and start to build a new and better foundation for their marriage?

_____

_____

_____

_____

_____

_____

_____

_____

_____

_____

LIFE APPLICATION

Fill in the blank diagram of the house with the key components of a healthy foundation for marriage found in this chapter.

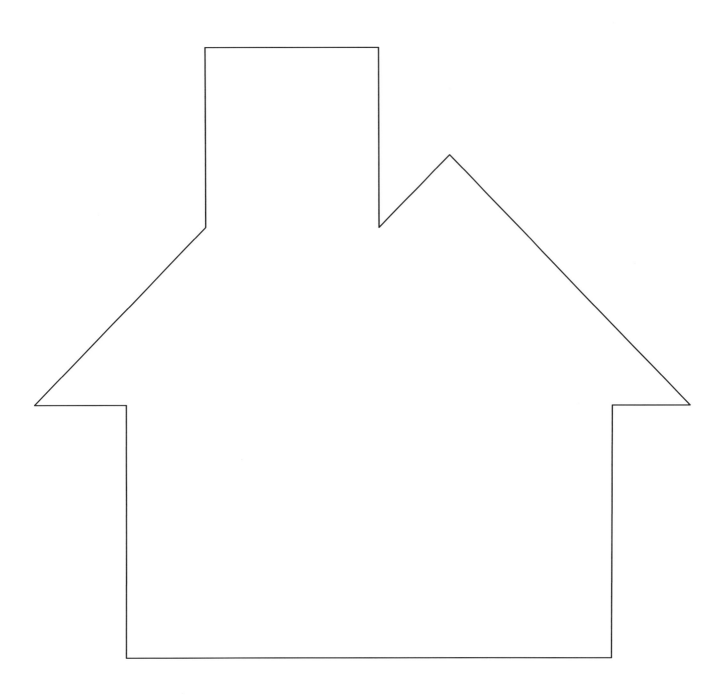

Reflections:

3

THE FOUR-GIVENESS FACTORS
Giving Grace God's Way

INTRO

Unforgiveness can lead to all sorts of problems in your marriage. Sometimes areas of unforgiveness are obvious and other times we hold things against our spouse without even realizing it. Even the littlest offense unforgiven can fester into a big problem over time. Unforgiveness can be a foothold wedging itself between you and your spouse. As unforgiveness is left unattended, that wedge is slowly hammered down driving you as a couple further and further apart.

In order to understand forgiveness, we think it is important to talk about what forgiveness is not. Forgiveness is not saying "what you did to me was okay" or "no big deal." Forgiveness is also not a reason to be drawn deeper into potentially harmful situations (like spousal abuse, repeated and unrepentant unfaithfulness, etc.). Instead, forgiveness is recognizing the fullness of someone's offense and fully releasing that debt to Jesus and what He did on the cross – Just like we expect Christ to do for us when we offend him. Furthermore, forgiveness is only the first step towards healing. Forgiveness opens the door for us as couples to grow beyond our mistakes. Without it, this growth is impossible.

In many situations, the forgiveness process can be difficult. At times, we want to forgive but do not know how to fully do so. Or at least, how to fully do so without repeatedly bringing up the matter and making our spouse "pay" for their mistake over and over again. Our marriage, like everyone else's, has given us several opportunities to learn how to properly forgive one another. We wish we could say we did it right every time, all the time, but we didn't. However, with prayer and practice, we started to work through the following four factors.

The First Factor: The Foundation

In Christ, we are able to surrender the offense to Him, and in the process, we can access his forgiving power for He is the foundation and genesis of all forgiveness. Making your marriage one of forgiveness requires that both you and your spouse turn to the cross in every situation, trusting in Jesus' grace and mercy to sustain you both. The reality is that our spouse is going to give us a reason to forgive them just about every day. Some days the offense will be big, other days small. The important thing is to work towards forgiveness in all places in your marriage. The Bible tells us to be kind and compassionate to one another, forgiving each other, just as Christ God forgave you.[4] It is only because of the mercy and grace that God extends to us every day that we are able to extend mercy and grace to one another. Thus, the first step in forgiveness is to set up Christ as the foundation for your marriage.

The Second Factor: Forgetting

You may have heard it said, "forgive but never forget." This can be a roadblock to forgiveness and is not the way that God deals with us Biblically speaking. Through Jesus' sacrifice for us on the cross, our sin is as far away as the East is from the West.[5] Do not hear us wrong; this isn't about pretending nothing ever happened and everything is okay. It is still important to work through painful offenses together for the sake of full reconciliation and healing. But allowing the thought of the offense to dominate your focus can be immensely damaging to a couple's intimacy on every level.

---

[4] *Be kind and compassionate to one another, forgiving each other, just as in Christ God forgave you. Ephesians 4:32*
[5] *He has removed our rebellious acts as far as the east is from the west, so far has he removed our transgressions from us. Psalm 103:12*

> ❝ I, even I, am he who blots out your transgressions, for my own sake, and remembers your sins no more.
> - Isaiah 43:25

Dwelling on the issue, bringing it up every day, and refusing to acknowledge any good your spouse has done are all subtle ways of choosing to not forget. This builds in you a sense of resentment and in your spouse a sense of shame. It can also create an unhealthy focus for our spouse on their failures. And as many of us know, if you focus on your failures… you tend to fail more. If we want to be champions in our marriage, we have to stop focusing on the misses.

So, what does it really look like to forget? And is forgetting really possible at all? Even though we cannot erase our memory, we can choose not to dwell on negative thoughts or thoughts that evoke negative emotions within us.

> ❝ We demolish arguments and every pretension that sets itself up against the knowledge of God, and we take captive every thought to make it obedient to Christ. - 2 Corinthians

Most of the time, it is not whether or not we can forget, but whether or not we want to forget. Holding something over our spouse's head can be a subtle and subconscious way of punishing them for the hurt they have caused us. This choice will only harm our marriage, ourselves, and our ability to move forward.

The Apostle Paul encourages us to follow his example as he forgets what is behind and to press on towards the goal that God had called him to.[6] Similarly, shifting your attention from the hurt that has happened to what God is calling you to in your marriage can bring healing and hope as the memory and sensitivity to the offense begin to fade. When a reminder comes up in your mind, bring it to the foot of the cross in surrender. We cannot afford to ruin our marriage because we cannot forget something. And when all else fails, think about a time you offended someone and wanted their forgiveness. We're all imperfect human beings and our expectation of each other should be that we will make mistakes because no one is perfect.

The Third Factor: Fighting For (Not Against)

If you saw your spouse being attacked by a group of people, would you join that group of people and kick your spouse while they were down? Of course not! Even if they did something to bring that beating upon themselves, we would still find a way to help them (and likely feel the need to call in reinforcements). Though this seems obvious, that sort of care doesn't usually seem to extend to our spouse when they are in a struggle that has caused them to hurt us.

Ephesians says that our fight is not against flesh and blood, aka, our spouse, but against the spiritual forces of evil in our world.[7] The devil and his evil spirits are not a fan of healthy marriage and forgiveness. He wants to make us view our spouse as the enemy so that we will work against one another. But it is not our job to go out and fight each other. Rather we are meant to be on the same team,

---

[6] *But one thing I do: Forgetting what is behind and straining toward what is ahead. I press on toward the goal to win the prize for which God has called me heavenward in Christ Jesus. Phillipians 3:13-14*
[7] *For our struggle is not against flesh and blood, but against the rulers, against the authorities, against the powers of this dark world and against the spiritual forces of evil in the heavenly realms. Ephesians 6:12*

fighting against our spiritual enemy who seeks to sabotage our relationship with each other and God.

God desires that we stop fighting with each other and start fighting for each other. What would it look like when we pray continually for them and with them, to shower over them the truth of who they are and the forgiveness that God offers them in Christ? This doesn't mean you cannot be mad, sad, or hurt by something your spouse has done. But it does matter how you respond to those emotions. It may help to ask, "What is my goal in this fight?" Are you simply fighting to be right? Are you trying to pay them back for what they have done? Or are you hoping to strengthen and support your spouse and your marriage? Are you turning to and seeking to honor God with the same fervor and energy you are using to respond to your hurt?

The Final Factor: Fortifying

A Godly marriage is the best antidote to changing and eradicating the ills of society and this world. As a result, the enemy will never get tired of attacking us repeatedly. It is not enough for us to fight off the enemy if we are not going to fortify our marriage against future attacks. And where will he attack? In the places where he has already found success.

The difficult part is that when we allow patterns of sin and hurt to run freely in our lives, habits begin to form that will not be easily broken. This is where our role as the one being forgiven really comes into play. It is not right for us to take advantage of our spouse's forgiveness by doing nothing to open ourselves to God's healing and transformation. It is important instead for us to be truly repentant (or to turn away from) in our sin against God and our spouse.

Repentance allows us to be open to changing the way we think.[8] To do this, we have to ask God, "Why am I going through this behavior again and again? What is it doing for me that I continue to seek it out, Lord?" You may find that you are looking at pornography as a way of experiencing false intimacy, or constantly tearing your spouse down because it helps you to feel powerful and in control. Bring these difficult truths to God knowing that there is no condemnation for those who are in Christ Jesus.[9] Ask Him, your spouse, and others in the Church community for help. You may even consider turning to a Christian counselor or a minister trained in pastoral care.

Once you have discovered the roots of this behavior, come up with a plan with your spouse to turn to God in those moments of need. This will undoubtedly require some change in the way you are living. As the age-old saying goes, "If nothing changes, nothing will change." Have an honest conversation together about what things are not helping and what things could. Make sure it is not all about simply stopping the behavior, but also finding things that strengthen your marriage for the better.

The Apostle Peter reminds us to "love each other deeply, because love covers over a multitude of sins" (1 Peter 4:8). We (Howard and Danielle) are not perfect people, but we know when push comes to shove, we have each other's back and are in this fight together. We are excited to explore what this looks like with you in more depth in the chapters to come.

---

[8] *Do not conform to the pattern of this world, but be transformed by the renewing of your mind. Then you will be able to test and approve what God's will is—his good, pleasing and perfect will. Romans 12:2*
[9] *Therefore, there is now no condemnation for those who are in Christ Jesus...Romans 8:*

PERSONAL REFLECTION

Take a few moments with yourself and God to write down the answer to the following question:

- Is there a behavior you continue to exhibit repeatedly, despite it having a negative influence on your marriage? How could you begin to truly repent of that behavior?

> **"** Love is patient, love is kind. It does not envy, it does not boast, it is not proud. It does not dishonor others, it is not self-seeking, it is not easily angered, it keeps no record of wrongs. - Corinthians 13:4-5

DISCUSSION QUESTIONS

Take some time to discuss the following questions as a couple or group:

- How does the world around us normally approach forgiveness? In what way is that different from the way God approaches forgiveness?

- What makes forgiveness so difficult? How can forgiving a spouse be uniquely difficult?

- Which of the four factors of forgiveness do you struggle with the most? How can implementing that factor help to bless your marriage?

- How can you strengthen your love for one another in marriage as a way of covering your spouse's sin as Christ's love covers yours? How are you investing in your marriage, your intimacy, and your love for one another?

HIS PERSPECTIVE

The very word forgiveness can be associated with emotions of disappointment, sadness, and anger, often because someone didn't live up to expectations. I, like most, entered my relationship with Danielle with expectations and marriage only heightened them. On a bad day, my wife has proven to be one of the most upstanding individuals I've encountered, which is why I call her God's favorite child. My admiration of her, however, can create a false sense of reality if not balanced with the proper perspective that she, like I, is imperfect and that's okay.

My mother told me during our engagement to treat our new marriage like an infant, and though I didn't have children at the time, I innately knew what she meant.

As wonderful and exciting as infants/children are, they are imperfect through their growth process. A mature parent understands that it's their commitment, patience, and grace that will aid in maturing that child, not a judgmental attitude of perfection. It would be silly to be harsh with a toddler who falls or fails; we intuitively and caringly pick them up and extend them grace. The same is true in marriage.

It became evident in our marriage that both of us would require the grace of the other to function confidently in a union that carries unrealistic expectations like no other. Grace is stronger than forgiveness because it extends undeserved favor to another person. Christ extended this grace through unconditional love, so who am I to not extend that to Danielle. I realize that grace carries with it different associations than forgiveness such as joy, peace, and pride; so I gladly strive to emulate my Savior in covering my wife with as much grace as possible.

HER PERSPECTIVE

I don't think I really knew much about true forgiveness until I got married. I'm not saying that Howard treated me so badly that I was given millions of chances to learn how to forgive. However, prior to marriage, I would normally just disassociate myself from a relationship or friendship if the person did or said something I didn't like. I would move on and tell myself, "I can forgive and not have to deal with you and that's okay." In reality, I was moving forward with the bitterness hidden in my heart because of that person's offense.

Obviously, in a healthy marriage, we don't really have the option of "fake-forgiveness" or disassociating ourselves from our spouse when they do something that rubs us the wrong way. For some reason (rooted in my childhood, I'm sure) I had a wall up shielding me from people that hurt or disappointed me. However, getting married challenged me to deal with those feelings. Since I couldn't run anymore, I began the process of actually learning how to work through the four steps of forgiveness mentioned in this chapter.

It also helped that Howard and I love to have fun and hang out. So being on each other's bad side and harboring unforgiveness took away from the overall excitement that comes with loving him for who he is. When I am able to accept that he is not perfect (and neither am I), I can let go of the offense and look forward to the happy days we have ahead.

CASE STUDY

Brenda was only married for two years before she noticed Teddy had a wandering eye. Brenda talked to him several times about how seeing him admire other women made her feel inadequate, but nothing changed. A short time later, Teddy called Brenda and said he had to work late one night and for her to not wait up for him. Brenda could tell in her gut something wasn't right and drove to Teddy's job. The night guard told Brenda that Teddy was not there and that he had left at his usual time. Brenda went back home and waited for Teddy to come home.

Around 3 a.m. Teddy came home and an argument erupted about where he had been and why he lied about needing to work late. After a long, exhausting night of going around and around with bits and pieces of the truth, Teddy finally confessed that he had been having an affair and was out with another woman. Even though Brenda was deeply hurt, she agreed to stay in the marriage and work on things while they went to counseling.

After a year in counseling, Brenda and Teddy started to believe that they could truly get past his affair and move on to brighter days ahead. Teddy did everything he could to prove to Brenda that he was a changed man and was committed to earning back her love, trust, and forgiveness. He gave her access to all of his social media accounts, emails and put a tracking device on his phone to show her he had nothing more to hide. However, every time they would have a little tiff, Brenda would bring up the affair.

One year passed, two years passed, three years passed and the affair was still all Brenda could talk about. Unfortunately, Brenda never really forgave Teddy, and after 8 years of still being berated for his affair and accused of cheating, even though he wasn't, Teddy filed for divorce. A few years later, Teddy met a new woman and got married, while Brenda was still single and blaming Teddy for her inability to trust men. Although Brenda would have been justified in divorcing Teddy, her decision to stay with him and truly offer forgiveness was the only way their marriage could have survived.

Discuss with your spouse (or your group) the takeaways from this case study. What went well, what went wrong? How could forgiveness have helped breathe new life into Brenda and Teddy's marriage? How is Brenda's unforgiveness still holding her prisoner even after her divorce?

_____

_____

_____

_____

_____

_____

LIFE APPLICATION

If there's anything that needs to be discussed in your marriage in the area of forgiveness, pray to God for the wisdom as to the proper timing and approach to discussing such things. Also, ask that God soften both of your hearts to hear and receive what your spouse is saying. When the timing is right, discuss with your spouse any area of unforgiveness you are harboring and ways you can work together to overcome these issues.

_____

_____

_____

Reflections:

4

THE SUBMISSION CYCLE:
Effectively Navigating Love & Respect

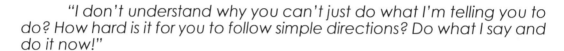

INTRO

"I don't understand why you can't just do what I'm telling you to do? How hard is it for you to follow simple directions? Do what I say and do it now!"

Whether this exchange is from a husband to a wife or from a wife to a husband, this is what most of us think of when we hear the word submission. Someone bossing us around in an unfriendly and unwelcoming tone, demanding action from us that we may or may not want to give. But we have to ask ourselves, what have we seen or experienced that has convinced us that this is what the word submission means? For some of us, nothing reminds us more of a nice fluffy doormat than this word. But dare we say the word gets a bad rap because we don't fully understand it in its biblical context?

Ephesians 5 calls all of us to submit to one another... woman to man and man to woman.[10] To submit is to *willfully* surrender control out of reverence and trust for another. This is key in understanding this passage. Jesus' submission is always intended to be a willful choice. Forced submission leads to relational abuse, something that is never God's will and is not something anyone is meant to endure.[11]

Biblical love is the other side of the same coin. To love is to *willfully* sacrifice everything for the betterment of another. Sometimes it may seem like the husband is getting the better end of this deal, but what is this passage really saying? The Bible says husbands are to love their wives *just as Christ loved the church and gave himself up for her.*[12] And how did Christ love His Church? He loved her to death, literally.

---

[10] *Submit to one another out of reverence for Christ. Ephesians 5:21*
[11] *If you are in an abusive relationship, find resources to help on page #*
[12] *Husbands, love your wives, just as Christ loved the church and gave himself up for her. Ephesians 5:25*

Disciple Your Wife Boldly

There is little doubt that Jesus loved His disciples dearly. Primarily, He did this by leading them and teaching them how to connect with the Father meaningfully. Jesus did this best by having His disciples follow Him closely and learn from His example. You are the spiritual leader of your family. And no one can follow you somewhere you're not going. This means, as a husband, discipling your wife is not so much a position of power over her, as it is a responsibility to her. Walking closely with Christ and leading your family to do the same is a vitally important part of loving your wife as Christ does.

Serve Your Wife Humbly

For Jesus, love was always defined by tangible acts of service, none more memorable than the washing of His disciples' feet. Washing feet was a job reserved for the lowest of servants and superseded comfort, position, and personal wellbeing. As a husband, it is this sort of humble service that you are to exemplify with your wife. This means you are to serve even in the ways that are difficult, unappealing, and may even feel beneath you for the sake of your wife feeling loved and served as the heir of Christ that she is. This means serving in both predictable (regular and expected) and unpredictable (special and unforeseen) ways.

Elevate Your Wife Sacrificially

Philippians 2 sums this up well:

> *In your relationships with one another, have the same mindset as Christ Jesus: Who, being in very nature God, did not consider equality with God something to be used to his own advantage; rather, he made himself nothing by taking the very nature of a servant, being made in human likeness. And being found in appearance as a man, he humbled himself by becoming obedient to death - even death on a cross! Philippians 2:5-8*

You are elevated as a husband so that you may elevate her as your wife. Practically, this means that you consider your wife's needs first in every decision you make. You are to lead your family with humility and strength, not using your leadership to benefit yourself first. Listen to her and regularly ask her opinion. Tell her why she is beautiful, strong, and admirable. Show her how she is lovable, respectable, and full of dignity. Encourage your wife daily with your words and actions, reminding her of her true identity and worth in Christ.

Lead Your Husband Patiently

Wives, you too have a spiritual role of leadership in your marriage. The Bible says a submitted wife can win over her unbelieving husband by her behavior... not by what she says.[13] Do not misunderstand, in no way is this passage meant to quiet you or to devalue your voice, but rather to demonstrate all the more the importance of your life with Christ. Your deep connection with our Lord and the life that overflows from it will be a testimony to your family of God and His goodness. Your patient and prayerful spiritual leadership in your marriage will send unfathomable ripples through your family for years to come.

---

[13] *Wives, in the same way, submit yourselves to your own husbands so that, if any of them do not believe the word, they may be won over without words by the behavior of their wives...1 Peter 3:1*

Respect Your Husband Courageously

Biblically speaking, respect means to honor and treat with reverence. The truth is, your husband (like us all) will not always be deserving of such veneration. In those moments, it is still important to offer your respect. In doing so, you call him to a higher standard of living and show him who God sees him as. Even if he won't say it, he longs for you as his wife to support him, trust him, and make him better.

> "Wives submit to your husbands, as is fitting for those who belong to the Lord. Husbands love your wives and never treat them harshly."
> - Colossians 3:18

This means:

1. Patiently supporting him in public, as well as lovingly challenging him in private.
2. Having his back and being his most trusted advisor.
3. Affirming him when he succeeds and encouraging him when he fails.
4. Being faithful, both physically and emotionally.
5. Being the one he can rely on, trust in, and go to for help and support.

Show him what the Lord thinks of him through the way you speak to, listen to, and treat him.

Believe in Your Husband Faithfully

One of the biggest things Christ asks of the Church is for us to faithfully believe in Him. This provides a helpful (and life-giving) model for a wife's belief in her husband. Your husband will not do everything perfectly and will certainly have doubts in his ability to lead, protect, and care for you and your family. It is vital for him that you believe in him more than he believes in himself. This is not always easy and takes great humility and release of control. But as you demonstrate your unwavering belief in him, it will awaken him to his deeper calling of trust and belief in God. This is a fundamental part of submission that we rarely think about, but is of huge importance.

Putting on the Eyes of Christ

If you both are committed to doing your part, each of you will continually feel elevated by the other in a cycle of submission and love, but this kind of love and submission is not easy. Familiarity with our spouse (in all the best and worst ways) can often lead to us taking him or her for granted. We can become underwhelmed in our marriage and feel like love and submission are a chore that we must carry out. In this, we have found it helpful to see our spouse as Christ sees them. This can spur on our curiosity about them and help us to reestablish that longing to know them more.

> " Don't be selfish; don't live to make a good impression on others. Be humble, thinking of others as better than yourself. – Philippians 2:3

Furthermore, Jesus shows deep unconditional love for each of us, and as we allow Him to love us, we become more and more lovable. When we love our spouse even when it is difficult to do so, we participate in Christ's transformation in their hearts. When we surrender power to our spouse willingly (as Christ does with us all), it helps them realize they are somebody worth trusting with such power. By seeing them with the eyes of Christ and treating them accordingly, we help to draw out in them who God has created them to be.

PERSONAL REFLECTION

Take a few moments with yourself and God to write down the answer to the following question:

- How well have you done up to this point at elevating your spouse? What is one practical way that you can better love them and submit to them?

DISCUSSION QUESTIONS

Take some time to discuss the following questions as a couple or with your group:

- What are some thoughts that come to mind when you hear the word "submission?" Where did this thought originate, and how do you feel about it now after reading the chapter?

- How can mutual submission help spouses to elevate one another in their marriage? What does it look like to willfully submit to one another out of reverence for Christ?

- In what ways do you feel most loved and respected? How do you personally want to love and respect your spouse better?

HIS PERSPECTIVE

Our wives are adults and deserve to be respected as such; it is from this perspective that I've gained Danielle's willful submission and have submitted myself to her as well (Ephesians 5:21). It is rare for a person to enjoy being told what to do simply because the rules say so, even a child desires a say in decision-making that impacts them. If the roles were reversed, I would dread the notion that my wife held the final say, not because she was deserving, but because "that's just the way it is." Empathizing with my wife caused me to work with her to create a democratic space in our home rather than a dictatorship. Because Danielle knows that I sincerely honor her insight as my partner, she , in turn, honors me with having the final say when necessary.

Truthfully, it is rare that we ever need to make "final say" decisions because I've learned that if my wife and I are not on one accord, it's typically best not to move forward. Remember, welcomed submission is an honor and privilege given for the services and sacrifices made by the one being submitted to. Being submitted to my Lord and Savior , Jesus Christ, has been the honor of my life because he has done so much for me. I am in service to Danielle, so that she may feel the same.

HER PERSPECTIVE

I think that men set the tone for how submission is received and carried out in the home. Howard has always treated me as an equal. He asks for my input on everything and shows me how I am valued in my role as his wife. Because he is so fair in this area and has never made me feel like it's his way or the highway, I take pleasure in letting him lead me. Our relationship has never been about either of us barking out orders or being harsh toward one another, so I choose to take the position of discussing a matter with him, but ultimately giving him the autonomy of making the decision and having the final say. Now with that said, the truth is that if we don't agree on a decision, we wait on making a decision. We pray and seek God until we're both at peace with whatever God is telling us to do. I understand that every relationship is different, but this is what works for..

CASE STUDY

Lee and Linda were married for one year when they came to us seeking advice on what submission is and how it should be carried out in their home. Lee worked at the local prison as a correctional officer and had been doing so for the past 12 years. He was a tall, burly man that could intimidate people just by his size. Day after day, Lee's job entailed maintaining the safety of the inmates and the institution. His duties required him to yell often, assert his authority, and command respect from those he was put in charge of, which sometimes led to physical altercations.

Lee was very well respected at his job and won numerous awards for his leadership style and ability to calm tense situations. Linda, on the other hand, was a manager at a pet shop and had a calm demeanor. She was short in stature and very thoughtful in her interactions with people. One day, as Lee and Linda were casually discussing different topics, Lee commented that he thought women should submit to men because women were the weaker vessel, and men didn't need the input from a woman to know what to do. Linda quickly discovered their views on submission were not aligned and pulled out the Bible. As they studied what the Bible said on submission, they learned that God expected them to submit to each other out of reverence for Christ. They both realized that man's headship discussed in the Bible meant sacrifice and responsibility, not superiority and control.

Discuss with your spouse (or your group) the takeaways from this case study. What went well, what went wrong? How could Lee and Linda's differing views on submission have created conflict in their marriage? How can understanding biblical submission help a marriage move forward in a far more healthy way?

LIFE APPLICATION

- Set aside some intentional time to study each other this week. Find out what you both like and dislike and how one another feels loved, so you are better equipped to serve one another.

Reflections:

5

WE-LINGUAL OR ME-LINGUAL?
Establishing Healthy & Effective Communication

INTRO

Have you ever been in an argument with your spouse and realized after the fact that they misunderstood something you were trying to say? Or misinterpreted your motive behind the words, which led to a bigger issue than you anticipated? Why does this happen? Here are two potential reasons: you have different communication styles and don't understand each other's language, or you are deliberately throwing darts with your words. Let's address the first issue: You and your spouse speak two different languages.

If you took a foreign language class in high school, you know how much goes into learning a new language and how freeing it is to be able to communicate with someone who speaks another tongue (even if just a little). In some ways, communicating with your spouse can be similar. Though it is unlikely that you and your partner literally speak two different languages, sometimes, however, it feels like you argue in Spanish while they yell back in French. In this case, neither person feels heard or understood, and your words can cause more harm than good.

This is because our communication history and styles are completely different. Both you and your spouse have different personalities, experiences, and outlooks on life. Each of you were shown different models of communication growing up, each with their own strengths and weaknesses. When we do not care to learn our partner's style, communication becomes self-centered, and we become focused only on getting our point across and saying what we want to say. Thus, understanding the way your spouse communicates is vital to the health of your marriage.

It is never too late to become a student of the way your partner communicates, so that you each can meet each other where you are at. It is helpful to learn how to make them smile, their areas of sensitivity, how often they expect to talk, what easily offends them, and when is a good (or bad) time to give feedback, to name a few. You can even ask questions like, "What is the best way to communicate to you that I love you?" or "How would you like me to respond to you when I am upset?" It is probably best to not bring these things up in the middle of an argument, but rather find a peaceful time to talk these things through. As you get the hang of it, you will learn to translate what you want to say into your partner's language.

It won't happen all at once, but when you both work to communicate in the other's language, you will find a more selfless communication emerge and that your spouse is more receptive to what you are saying. This is the basis for communicating from a place of love and respect. And over time, a language unique to your marriage will emerge, one rooted in God's plan for your relationship.

> " My dear brothers and sisters, take note of this: Everyone should be quick to listen, slow to speak and slow to become angry... - James 1:19

More Than Words Can Say

It is well known that a large portion of communication is nonverbal. Tone, posture, approach, gestures, expressive sounds, eye movements, facial expressions, and the like, all contribute to what we are trying to communicate. Even our timing and how often we bring something up sends a message. Our brains automatically filter what is being said through these nonverbal cues to better interpret what is being communicated.

Depending on how these cues are being used, they can greatly assist or hinder your communication. When these non-verbals go unchecked, things can get nasty quick and all sorts of unhealthy communication can be stirred up.[14] For example, our default might be to raise our voice or become passive-aggressive when we are hurt by something our spouse has said or done. We want to communicate our hurt but instead, end up pushing our spouse further away because harsh words make tempers flare. Therefore, it is good to consider your approach when communicating with your spouse.

Your approach describes all of what is being communicated beyond the words you are saying. Identify what you want to say and ask yourself, "How can I best get this message across in a loving and respectful way?" It may require you to turn off the TV, put down your phone, make eye contact, and adopt a non-combative posture. Consider the best way to phrase what you want to say and how your tone will be interpreted. A demand made harshly is not as effective as a request made calmly. Spend time listening to their perspective; this shows how you value them and what they have to say. Becoming disciplined in your nonverbal communication can go a long way in building a healthy marriage.

---

[14] *A gentle answer turns away wrath, but a harsh word stirs up anger. Proverbs 15:1*

Words of Life

Our choice of words can either speak life to a situation or usher in the death of it.[15] Sometimes we do not consider the impact that our words can have on our spouse. Offhand comments, half-serious jokes, regular criticism, and unkind words can all speak death into the heart of our spouse. On the other hand, it is normal to brush aside opportunities to affirm, encourage, and uplift your husband or wife with words of life. Here is a question that may require each of us to take an honest look in the mirror: Where are these words of death coming from?

When couples tell us they have "communication" problems, we often find that there is a deeper heart-issue that is only surfacing through the couple's hurtful communication.[16] Unresolved conflict, unforgiveness, pride, inability to hold one's temper, and unbridled stress can all lead to verbal jabs towards one's partner. These unaddressed heart-issues not only spew words of death, but they also choke out our words of life.

By limiting destructive language and maximizing life-giving words in your marriage, you will see God's healing start to flow through your communication.

> " Though many issues can be resolved with the healthy communication practices outlined here, some issues are better served with a trained counselor or therapist. There is no shame in this. Reach out to your local church or check out the American Association for Marriage and Family Therapy (aamft.org) to locate help near you.

---

[15] *The power of life and death is in the tongue. Proverbs 18:21a*
[16] *The mouth speaks what the heart is full of. Matthew 12:34b*

PERSONAL REFLECTION

Take a few moments with yourself and God to write down the answer to the following question:

- How am I speaking words of death to my spouse? What unresolved heart-issues might these words be overflowing from?

_____

_____

_____

_____

DISCUSSION QUESTIONS

Take some time to read this scripture and discuss these questions as a group:

" Do not let any unwholesome talk come out of your mouths, but only what is helpful for building others up according to their needs, that it may benefit those who listen. - Ephesians 4:29

- What are some examples of unhealthy communication patterns and habits that people display in the marriage relationship?

- Based on the verse above, what do you think makes talk unwholesome? What unresolved heart-issues might these words be overflowing from?

- How can we communicate our passionate feelings in a way that is loving and respectful? When do my spouse and I at times speak different languages?

- In what areas does my spouse need me to speak words of life and encouragement?

HIS PERSPECTIVE

At the onset of our relationship, Danielle and I really struggled in our communication, primarily because we began dating at an early age, and our conversations reflected the environments that we were raised in. I come from a long lineage of great domestic debaters, whose simple discussions could easily turn into an argument about right and wrong, and I adopted that style in our relationship. Quickly, I realized that I was always arguing with the person I enjoyed the most and our quality time was limited because of it. Danielle began to constructively make me aware of my competitive communication style and how she received it, which aided in me making a change for the greater good. I've learned in our marriage to not communicate through the lens of right and wrong because you can be right and dead wrong at the same time!

Danielle and I also discovered that what we thought was a communication problem, was truly a temperament problem that contaminated our conversation. The Bible says that a "soft answer turns away wrath" (Proverbs 15:1), but we both found it difficult not to verbally "jab" each other, which almost always escalated into arguments. All too often, our tempers would flare up, cause us to become defensive, and lead to disrespectful and regrettable communication. It wasn't until we learned how to "hold it and fold it" (aka choose your battles) and "count down before you blast off" (aka think before you speak) that we developed the proper self-control to effectively and lovingly communicate.

HER PERSPECTIVE

When Howard and I first started dating, I remember speaking to him in the manner and tone I'd seen my parents speak to each other while I was growing up. Naturally, as a young 19-year-old, I thought this was how everyone spoke to each other in relationships and that it was acceptable. After a few serious arguments, I quickly learned that if our relationship was going to work, I had to learn how to talk to Howard in a way and tone that he could receive and feel respected by.

Later on, years into our marriage and my career as a Probation Officer, Howard and I had another heart to heart about my style of communication towards him. In my mind, I was no longer talking to him crazy, so all should have been well. However, he brought to my attention that since I was used to telling people what to do all day in a very direct manner, that I had started talking to him the same way! It wasn't my intention by any means, but I'm thankful that we created an environment earlier on that allowed us to call each other out when we felt uncomfortable with the way the other was acting or communicating.

CASE STUDY

Early in their marriage, Devin and Tracy argued a lot. Devin felt like Tracy constantly disrespected him by talking down to him and assuming he couldn't do anything right without her input. During several arguments, Devin would remind Tracy that he was an adult, just like she was, and he took care of himself without incident prior to ever meeting her. Tracy, on the other hand, felt like Devin couldn't do anything right, and she felt compelled to help him so he wouldn't embarrass himself or her.

After their first five years of marriage, things quieted down, but Tracy noticed that Devin stopped talking to her about things –big things, small things, and even everyday current events. Devin was quiet about pretty much everything these days. She asked him over and over again why he stopped talking to her and had seemed to "check out," but Devin never really had an answer. Not only had Devin stopped talking to Tracy, but he also seemed uninterested in spending time with her and their intimacy was suffering. Tracy decided to set up a counseling appointment to find out what went wrong in their marriage. Devin explained to the counselor their communication history and how her disrespect and inability to speak his language made him feel like she didn't care about him or value him as a man.

Discuss with your spouse (or group) the takeaways from this case study. What went well, what went wrong? How could Devin and Tracy's differing views on how to speak to each other have created conflict in their marriage?

LIFE APPLICATION

If your communication challenge is speaking a different language: Take turns listening to each other for 3-5 minutes. The spouse that was initially quiet and listening, then sums up what they believe they heard and what they would deem the most important aspects of the conversation were to their spouse. Then switch turns and repeat the activity.

_____

_____

_____

If your communication challenge is attacking each other with unloving words: Make a list of any hurtful or disrespectful words/labels your spouse has directed toward you and explain how it has made you feel. It is the job of each spouse to be quiet and listen...not to argue or debate the truth of the matter. At the end of the exercise, both spouses (or the offending spouse) make a vow to no longer use those words/labels expressed in the exercise.

_____

_____

_____

Reflections:

6

FOREVER FRIENDS
Building a Friendship That Lasts

INTRO

In the early years of our relationship, we were most excited about developing our friendship with each other and focusing on how much fun we had together. That friendship built a foundation for us to enjoy our marriage and know that we had each other's backs no matter what. It wasn't always easy, but choosing to be best friends has helped us to weather storms and continue to be there for each other unconditionally.

Sometimes while coaching other couples, we will hear, "I love you, but I don't like you." Though no marriage is without its struggles, settling for friendshipless marriage like this is not what God has in mind for you. Your spouse becoming your best friend means they are the person that you like the most, would do anything for, and want to spend the most time with.

For some of you, this may feel far off, but there is no need to feel discouraged. Becoming best friends is not something you simply stumble into or that grows through osmosis. It is a choice that takes intention and time.

Making the Choice

Many marriages, including yours, probably began as friendships. You couldn't get enough of each other, wanted to do everything together, and know everything about each other. But as time goes on and the commitment gets bigger, friendships often fade in favor of being... well, just married. That may sound a little bit funny, but a marriage without friendship is like a sail without wind. It can look big, impressive and powerful; but at the end of the day, it is going nowhere and you may eventually be tempted to abandon ship. What does it look like to truly keep that friendship going or perhaps reignite a friendship that has lost steam?

The first step in any friendship is making the choice to actually be friends. Though they might not deserve the title or have not done anything lately to indicate this level of friendship, without first making the choice to be best friends, you will not get far. In this, we are following Jesus' lead who, though we do not deserve it, calls us friends[17] and demonstrated true loving friendship by laying his life down for us.[18] Jesus made the choice to be our friend no matter what and then acted as only a friend could.

For us, this is a choice that we will have to make every day for our spouse. Some days it will be easier, other days it will be more difficult. But your spouse needs to know that you are with them and you choose them. When you make this choice, your spouse is no longer conditional to you. Like Jesus, you eradicate the qualifications and say, "you are my best friend, no matter what."

---

[17] ...Instead, I have called you friends, for everything that I learned from my Father I have made known to you. John 15:15b
[18] Greater love has no one than this: to lay down one's life for one's friends. John 15:13

It is not enough to simply say you are best friends and then do nothing to help that become a reality, though. It is important to define what you both want the friendship to be. What kinds of things do you want to do together? What intentional choices will you make to create the bonds that will sustain your friendship? What does a best friendship really look like and how do you want to replicate that at home? How do you want to relate and connect to each other in day-to-day life? What (outside of your kids) is going to be the glue that keeps you coming back to one another? Will you institute a weekly date night? Or go on a trip – just the two of you? Will you find activities that you like to do together? These little choices can make a huge difference in your friendship with your spouse.

Becoming Good Company

As we mentioned before, you cannot become the best friends you want to be without spending regular, intentional time together. Often in marriage, we allow our differences to hold us apart, and thus we rarely come together. This is not to say that you should not have time to yourself or with other friends, but when you find all of your fun and friendship outside of your spouse, it can create a small invisible divot in your relationship. As time goes on, you get used to being separated from one another and find most of your joy apart from your spouse. This can open the doors to marital unhappiness, loss of intimacy, and at times unfaithfulness.

Though that behavior is never justified, it does highlight how spending time together in a joy-filled friendship is a very big deal.

It is vital then for you to find common ground and learn what it means to become "good company" for your spouse. This means that you take the time to intentionally learn who they are and how they are changing. Stay in touch with their likes and dislikes. Do research about their interests. Learn to appreciate what they appreciate. Go out of your way to engage in hobbies that they like. It is not that you have to be interested in those things, so much as being actually interested in your spouse.

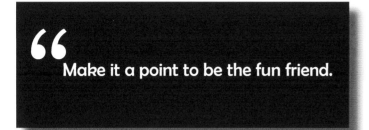

> **Make it a point to be the fun friend.**

These little choices each day go far beyond simply being into the same things. It communicates how much you are into them. By engaging with your spouse this way, you help to show them (consciously and subconsciously) that you care for them, you highly esteem them, and that your loyalty lies with them. These little things may not make a huge impact right away, but as you invest in each other bit by bit and gain this common ground, you will be drawn together more and more.

This may mean becoming a fan of their favorite sports team or going to a concert of their favorite band or artist. It could look like reading the same book and talking about it or going out on dates that are fun for them. No matter what it is, do things together with a positive attitude and the joy of getting to be with your best friend.[19] We all fall into the trap of not letting ourselves have fun by being overly critical or constantly negative. Your spouse can tell when you are not into it, and it communicates that "I am not into this time with you." When we act this way, it makes us not fun to be around. Sometimes the difference between being "the fun friend" and being "a downer" is simply approaching time with your spouse with excitement and positivity.

---

[19] *Do everything without grumbling or arguing. Philippians 2:14*

Taking the Pressure Off

Finally, an important part of friendship can be taking the pressure off of one another. When our expectations of one another in marriage reach an unhealthy level, it can feel a lot like a tightrope. One wrong step and we fear falling to our death. As a result, we often feel paralyzed and unable to approach one another for fear of doing something that will offend our spouse and ultimately hurt our marriage. In this "walking on eggshells" state, friendship is simply not possible.

As strange as this may sound, there are moments that we should approach each other as friends before we approach each other as spouses. When things get difficult between the two of you, it can become important to mentally take a step down from the role of husband or wife and look for ways to help your spouse as you would a friend. This is because friendship doesn't necessarily come with all the expectations that marriage comes with. As friends, you are often more free to be imperfect. It becomes easier to approach them with compassion, care, and forgiveness.

This doesn't mean that you have no expectations or that you minimize major issues (you will still have to work through these things). It just means letting your spouse know that you are willing to work through it together. You are communicating to them, "You don't have to worry about being perfect. I love you for who you are, not what you do." In this, friendship can become a safety net so that you can catch each other when you fall.

It is key that you do not wait around for your spouse to act first, but that you both take the initiative. It starts with you making the choice to invest in your spouse in a special way and to allow God to shape and guide you in your friendship with one another. Then we can take the pressure off and ultimately shift our expectations towards God and His good and joy-filled plan for our marriage.

PERSONAL REFLECTION

Take a few moments with yourself and God to write down the answer to the following question:

- What first got you excited about your friendship with your spouse? How are you still investing in that friendship and how might you be neglecting it?

_____

_____

_____

_____

> ❝ "A man who has friends must himself be friendly; but there is a friend who sticks closer than a brother."- Proverbs 18:24

DISCUSSION QUESTIONS

Take some time to discuss the following questions as a couple or group:

- Who have you seen demonstrate how to be best friends with a spouse well? What have you seen them do to invest in this friendship?

_____

_____

- How can being unintentional with your friendship to your spouse lead to a disconnect in your relationship?

_____

_____

- What are you both hoping for in your friendship with your spouse? How do you want to show up in a new and purposeful way in this friendship?

_____

_____

- What could it look like to create an intimate friendship around special activities and interests that your spouse likes?

_____

_____

HIS PERSPECTIVE

Typically, we befriend someone because we like certain things about them, enough to want to be around them. Danielle and I were friends first. I really liked her, and though this may sound overly simple or less than romantic, it has been the secret sauce in our 19-year relationship. Frequently, I hear spouses mention how they "love their spouse, but don't like them" and I am sincerely saddened by the reality of someone not liking a person they live with for an extended period of time. Genuinely liking Danielle is what makes me want to weather the seasonal patterns of romance, health, finance, and vanity. In fact, because Danielle is my best friend, I'm purposeful in weathering stormy seasons in our marriage, so I can get back to enjoying life with her. Don't let Satan, who hates marriage, cause you to hate the spouse you once liked so much!

> **"Greater love has no one than this: to lay down one's life for one's friends. - John 15:13**

HER PERSPECTIVE

As we stated at the beginning of this chapter, when Howard and I first began dating, we did everything together...whether I liked it or not and whether he liked it or not. We didn't care where we were going, where we were eating, or what was on the agenda, we just knew we wanted to be together and could make a good time out of anything. However, as time went on, I wasn't really interested in certain things he wanted to do... like attending professional basketball games and going to the movies. I still wanted to spend time with him, but I wanted to spend it doing what I enjoyed doing!

After several conversations, it dawned on me that he had his interests prior to us getting together and that I should partake in whatever made him happy, just like he happily obliged to do or go to where ever made me happy. I even noticed that whatever I was interested in at the moment, he would jump in headfirst. I had an interest in learning how to sew, he suggested I sign up for a sewing class at the local community college and bought me a sewing machine. I had an interest in growing vegetables in our backyard, he bought me a greenhouse. Then, I became obsessed with the "natural hair" movement, he spent hours upon hours watching YouTube videos with me and listening to me explain what stage my hair was in... for four long years.

Did he care about sewing, growing vegetables, or what I was doing with my hair? No! But he made it a point to include himself so that we could have conversations and outings centered around my interests. If you're wondering if I ever returned the favor... I did. I started buying tickets to NBA games as our budget permitted and studying up on players, trade deals, and the latest news on his favorite teams. In essence, I made it a point to become the fun friend.

CASE STUDY

Laura and John started off their relationship spending a lot of time together hanging out and getting to know each other through the hobbies each one was interested in. They would go to new places, try new restaurants, see plays, go to sports games and overall just have a blast. Once they got married, however, going out took a backseat to careers, bills, and children, and before long, they weren't doing much together. Laura used to be the funniest person to John and now it seemed like she was just happy with staying at home and watching television.

Tina, John's partner at work (who happened to be single), was outgoing, spontaneous and everyone loved her. John and Tina worked well together on their projects and soon started having lunch together. Tina won tickets to a basketball game on the radio for John's favorite team and invited him and another coworker to go with her… as friends, of course. John initially de-clined, but then thought about how he and Laura never did anything exciting anymore and decided why not! John lied to Laura and told her he was working late, when in reality, he was at the basketball game.

When he got home and saw Laura, he felt guilty for lying and going out to have fun without her, so he decided to tell Laura the truth. She was very upset with him, and a major argument ensued, ending in Laura going to bed by herself. Though she was hurt, she couldn't stop thinking about how she used to like having fun and going out with John but hadn't really felt up to it for the last few years. She examined what had taken her interest and started to feel guilty that John felt he had to sneak around just to have fun. After a few nights of prayer and silence, Laura talked to John about how she was hurt by his decision but also apologized to John for her role in abandoning their friendship.

Discuss with your spouse (or group) the takeaways from this case study. How could John and Laura have better navigated this scenario both individually and as a couple?

LIFE APPLICATION

It is important for spouses to spend time alone, undistracted by work, kids, and other obligations; therefore, we recommend implementing a weekly date night (if you don't already have one). To come up with new, fresh ideas, each spouse should write down on 5 slips of paper the 5 activities they would love to do, places they would like to go, restaurants they would like to try, etc., and place them in a jar. When date night comes up, pick an activity from the jar and try something new together. Even if it is just coffee at your kitchen table after the kids go to sleep, it is an important habit in building your friendship!

Reflections:

7

MONEY MATTERS:
Managing Finances Like a Team

INTRO

Many times, couples enter into marriage with differing views on the topic of money. Some talk about their future expectations on how it should be managed, who will do the managing, if they will share a bank account... and some don't. We came into our marriage thinking that how we've managed our money when we were single was automatically good enough to carry over into marriage. However, we learned quickly that not being in alignment with each other on how to manage the finances could open the door for evil to sneak in through the back door and use money to destroy our marriage.

Making the Choice

The front wheels of a car are used to steer and guide the vehicle in one direction or another. When the wheels are misaligned, it can cause a lot of problems with the steering of the car. In our own experience and talking to others we have worked with, one of the main challenges with finances in marriage is misalignment. Misaligned couples tend to seek monetary control and independence from one another. It may or may not surprise you that many couples keep their finances separate even in marriage, with individual (and at times secret) bank accounts. These "rainy day" or "free reign" accounts (though seeming to make practical sense) are in fact harmful to the trust of your marriage and create a divisive wedge between you and your spouse. It communicates to your spouse that they cannot be trusted and that you have a backup plan in case you need to "jump ship."

> **" Money is an opportunity to reach unity in marriage. When couples work together, they can do anything. - Unknown**

Though it may feel difficult at first, we encourage couples to seek alignment in their finances as a part of the oneness they share in marriage. The kind of oneness that God encourages means that you both understand that all your money, wealth, and possessions belong to both of you together, and even before that, belong to God. He has given us everything and made us stewards of all we have. He desires that our money be used not just for our own good but for the good of others and His Kingdom. This will require you asking, "God, how can we love you and others with what you have given us?"

In this stewardship, you both are a team and have an equal amount of say and responsibility in the way money is used. The "breadwinner" does not then have the authority to make all the decisions, nor should one spouse do whatever they want without considering the other. Savers and spenders both have to be willing to bend without demonizing or judging the other person. Alignment requires prayer, conversation, and compromise. You will have to get on the same page with one another and with God in order to start moving in the same direction.

It is a best practice to decide together on rules and boundaries to help keep alignment with and account-ability to one another. It is important to find ways to be completely transparent with each other, setting spending limits, talking through big purchases, and having all your bank accounts and credit cards completely shared. Only then can you start to bring your finances under your own shared authority and under God's authority.

> **Married couples, don't be discouraged if you are misaligned. It is unrealistic to think that you will have this conversation once and never again. Every car after a while needs a tire alignment and so will you!**

Have Vision and Purpose

Something that is extremely helpful to the alignment of your finances is to have a shared purpose and vision for your money. Purpose and vision can act as a compass, helping to bring you both back on the same path when things become out of focus. This can only come if you decide together what your shared goals are for your finances.[20]

Deciding on this shared vision and purpose requires buy-in from you both. When you both are not bought into the same vision and purpose for your money, it is easy to feel like your spouse is wasting it. It is important to spend time together praying, talking and considering what you both want to do with the money you have been given, and what God would have you do with it. This vision should involve larger life-long goals (saving for a child or their college fund, putting money away for retirement, having enough to always support those in need, etc.) and smaller short-term goals (saving for a new car, a vacation or to go on a mission trip with your church).

---

[20] *Can two walk together unless they are agreed? Amos 3:3*

Once you have agreed upon your goals together, you are better prepared as a couple to make wise and responsible decisions that respect and consider one another. Though you may have the ability in a given moment to buy something out of alignment, you have decided together that the money you have isn't for that purpose. Instead, it becomes much more clear when to say no to a purchase or lovingly hold each other accountable when you are misaligned. In many ways, laying out the vision for your money is a practice in delayed gratification. It is building the discipline to say "no" to unnecessary things now, so that you can say "yes" to the things you have decided are truly important to you both and are important to God.

> ❝ Engaged couples, you should have this conversation before getting married - to start your marriage off with a sense of the other person's financial perspective and habits.

Take Responsibility

When it comes to managing your money as a team, it is crucial that you both take financial responsibility for the wellbeing of your marriage and family. Both you and your spouse have to do all you can to not "let the ship sink" financially, so to speak. When water is pouring in and the ship begins to sink, we as spouses have a responsibility to each other to do our part. Often we can allow pride, foolishness, irresponsibility, and selfishness to rip a hole in the hull of our finances and put our families in jeopardy. This can mean taking on a second job or letting go of building a dream business so that your family can stay afloat in times of need.

Spiritual ignorance or arrogance can also be a problem, causing us to believe that God hasn't called us to "that job" or "that way of living." But our first ministry in God's eyes is always to care for our spouse and family. Even the Apostle Paul, who wrote most of the New Testament, had a job making tents while doing his ministry. He had a profession to take care of himself and those around him, though it wasn't his primary calling. We need to have each other's back, and each of us must make sacrifices at different times if we are truly to support one another and take responsibility for what we have been given.

In marriage, God does not see us as separate but as two individuals choosing to live as one.

PERSONAL REFLECTION

Take a few moments with yourself and God to write down the answer to the following question:

- In what ways are you and your spouse financially aligned, and where could you use an alignment?

DISCUSSION QUESTIONS

❝❝ **Do not store up for yourselves treasures on earth, where moths and vermin destroy, and where thieves break in and steal. But store up for yourselves treasures in heaven, where moths and vermin do not destroy, and where thieves do not break in and steal. For where your treasure is, there your heart will be also. - Matthew 6:19-21**

Take some time to discuss the following questions as a group:

- Why do you think discussing money is such a sensitive issue? How have you seen money be a conflict among couples who are misaligned?

  _____

  _____

- What do you think it means when Jesus says "where your treasure is, there your heart will be also?" How can a couple work as a team to "store up treasures in heaven?"

  _____

  _____

- What vision and purpose do you want for your finances as a couple? How can you both seek better alignment in that vision?

  _____

  _____

- How might God be calling you to use your finances as a couple? How can you both take responsibility for your finances and fund what God is calling you to?

  _____

  _____

HIS PERSPECTIVE

Proverbs 16:18 tells us, "pride goes before destruction and arrogance before a fall." When Danielle and I got married and began to govern all our finances together and with complete transparency (highly recommended), I had to humble myself and come under her leadership with our finances. She had a stronger background in financial management, and in turn, became the CFO of our marriage. (Every marriage needs a chief financial officer as a check and balance to a mutually agreed-upon financial strategy). Just remember that though one spouse may be designated as the CFO, both spouses should be respected as equal owners when financial decisions are being made.

HER PERSPECTIVE

When Howard and I were dating, we were young, in college, and broke. We both had minimum wage jobs and put our little coins together to hang out, go places, and eat fast food. The thought of how we actually spent our money, or what our attitudes toward money management were, never came up as a topic of conversation. Once we got married, I quickly noticed that we were different in this area. Growing up I saw two sets of spending patterns. One parent was a saver and the other was a spender. I took after the saver. So much so that I was frugal to a default, which later turned out to be detrimental in some areas of our marriage. For instance, spending money for a date night would bother me.

Nevertheless, since we had an open dialogue type relationship, we were never afraid to discuss money, our bills, or how we could create a budget, income goals or anything else. Howard saw that I was pretty decent with our money and allowed me to take the reins in being our family's chief financial officer. He is (and was) very hands-on and knowledgeable regarding our financial affairs and this has allowed for transparency and accountability.

CASE STUDY

Margot and Steve didn't get married until their late 30s. Therefore, they were both set in their financial ways and neither had plans to change themselves or to try to change the other. Their agreement was that Margot would keep her account and Steve would keep his account, and they would open a joint account together. Their bills would remain separate, but Steve would pay for the mortgage out of his account, and Margot would pay for the utilities and her credit card out of her account. They never really discussed bills with the exception of an occasional reminder here and there. Steve usually got home from work first and would always check the mail. One week while Steve was out of town, Margot checked the mail and noticed there was a default letter from their mortgage company demanding payment for the past three months! In shock, Margot called Steve to find out why he hadn't paid the mortgage, at which time, Steve confessed that he had lost his job and didn't want to scare Margot because he was in the process of looking for another job.

Discuss with your spouse (or group) the takeaways from this case study. How could seeking alignment and creating a household vision and purpose have better equipped Margot and Steve to deal with their financial matters?

_____

_____

_____

_____

_____

_____

_____

LIFE APPLICATION

Each of you should separately write out the "why" behind what you believe to be the financial values of your marriage. When you are both done, trade papers and highlight the positives of your spouse's approach to finances. Afterward, discuss and write down what you want to be your shared financial values as a couple.

_____

_____

_____

Reflections:

8

A HOLISTIC CONNECTION
Three Essentials to Intimacy

INTRO

Intimacy, in its various forms, is so important when it comes to your marriage. To be intimate with someone is to be fully known by that person. To be exposed. To be open to receiving love while at the same time open to receiving threat. There are different levels of intimacy and we are meant to share the deepest levels with those we trust most. The level of intimacy you experience with someone will be directly connected with the trust you have built with that person. Acquaintances will not know you as well as your close friends and family.

Throughout the years, we have seen many couples struggle to trust each other fully when it comes to the most vulnerable parts of themselves. Usually, this stems from the fear that if we are fully known, we will not be loved. A lack of intimacy in a marriage creates major problems and can prevent your marriage from thriving the way God desires it to. Husbands and wives feel a sense of distance between one another and do not feel fully understood. When neglected, intimacy issues can contribute greatly to boredom, resentment, and unfaithfulness in a marriage. In response to this, we want to take a closer look at three kinds of intimacy and how to better experience them in your marriage.

Physical Intimacy

From hand holding to hugging, high-fives to a kiss, physical connection is something we deeply crave as humans. God set us up to connect this way and it is a big part of what he has in mind for you and your spouse. We like to think about it as an act of remembrance, reminding us of our oneness and connectedness in marriage.

There is little in this world that is as intimate as sex, and the bond that is built through it is indispensable to a marriage. Sadly, a healthy sex life is becoming more and more rare in the marriage relationship. Current portrayals of sex expressed in pop culture, pornography, and promiscuous lifestyles, create unhealthy images of what sex is like and what it is used for. While our society considers sexual connection "not a big deal," using this intimate act as a means of conquest or control is becoming the norm.[21] As a result, some view it as unessential to marriage, while others secretly harbor resentment because of how little they connect sexually. Sexual rejection leaves some wondering if their spouse still desires them, while sexual pressure makes others feel objectified.

This is why it is so important to fight for a healthy sex life in your marriage, the secret of which is selfless love. When sex is first about pleasing and expressing love to your spouse, it takes a turn for the better. You do not have to worry about yourself because you trust your spouse has your best interest in mind and vice versa. Sex with your spouse is the ultimate unspoken compliment, intended to communicate the highest level of love, esteem, and longing. Both spouses are required to trust each other in order not to be vulnerable. Your spouse offering themselves in this way should not be taken lightly. Both men and women should be conscious of what makes their spouse feel safe, cared for, and pleased during sex and make a conscious effort to connect regularly in this way. How frequently "regular" is, should be a mutual determination between you and your spouse.[22]

---

[21] *The wife gives authority over her body to her husband, and the husband gives authority over his body to his wife. 1 Corinthians 7:4*
[22] *Do not deprive each other except perhaps by mutual consent and for a time, so that you may devote yourselves to prayer. Then come together again so that Satan will not tempt you because of your lack of self-control. 1 Corinthians 7:5*

Emotional Intimacy

Another important part of intimacy in marriage is emotional connectedness. The powerful draw to connect with someone's inner self is in some cases, stronger than their sex drive. An imbalance of physical connectedness without care for the emotional core of your spouse can lead them to feel uninteresting and used. For some, this means providing a safe space for your spouse to share their thoughts and feelings, and trusting them enough to open up about yours. For others, this will feel even more vulnerable and terrifying than opening up physically. Allow your spouse to ease into sharing this part of themselves to show them you can be trusted.

There are many intimacy killers in marriage. So many that we can't discuss them all here. However, one common way we see the most in counseling couples is breaking your spouse's confidentiality. When you share the intimate details of your spouse's inner world, sexual preferences, or shortcomings with others, it is a breach of their trust. Even if you think your spouse will never find out, think about how you would feel if the shoe was on the other foot. Another way to negatively impact your emotional connection is by having an affair. Similar to physical unfaithfulness, emotional affairs can feel like a huge betrayal to your spouse. Some couples and experts alike even argue that emotional affairs are worse

than physical affairs due to the fact that emotional affairs create a bond that sometimes isn't there in physical affairs. There should be a level of emotional intimacy that is reserved only for them. If breaches like these are made, building new trust will require you both to work together towards forgiveness and repentance, and it may take some time to create a new normal of trustness and repentance, and it may take some time to create a new normal of trust.

> **You shall not commit adultery. - Exodus 20:14**

Spiritual Intimacy

As we wrote about in previous chapters, a spiritual connectedness of a husband and wife is vital for a healthy marriage. We like to call it the "Secret Sauce" to healthy intimacy. Even those that have strong relationships with God can allow this area of connectedness to go unnoticed for extended periods of time. Unfortunately, it is not something you can manufacture in a time of crisis or when you need it most. You will receive from this connection what you put into it. Making a regular habit of praying, sharing from your heart, and reading God's word with your spouse can have a massive impact on the long-term health of your marriage.

Like other forms of intimacy, the depths of your spiritual life should be reserved first for God and second for your spouse. This doesn't mean that you cannot have a deep spiritual connection with others. But there should be a level of spiritual intimacy set aside just for your husband or wife. If you are constantly praying with and inviting a specific person into the depths of that space beside your spouse, it can create an unhealthy dependence. It could be helpful to talk through with your spouse the boundaries you want to set up to protect your marriage and foster the best spiritual intimacy.

PERSONAL REFLECTION

Take a few moments with yourself and God to write down the answer to the following question:

• What area of intimacy is it most difficult for you to connect with your spouse? In what ways do you long for more intimacy in your marriage?

DISCUSSION QUESTIONS

Take some time to discuss the following questions as a couple or group:

66 **The man said, "This is now bone of my bones and flesh of my flesh; she shall be called 'woman,' for she was taken out of man." That is why a man leaves his father and mother and is united to his wife, and they become one flesh. Adam and his wife were both naked, and they felt no shame. Genesis 2:23-25**

- How is the Biblical approach to intimacy different from the way the world treats intimacy? In what ways do you see our world misunderstand the various areas of intimacy (physical, emotional, and spiritual)?

- How is the nakedness of Adam and his wife important to understanding intimacy? What do you think is significant about them feeling no shame?

- What do you think it would be like to be naked in every way with your spouse? How would it benefit your marriage, and how would it be a challenge for you both?

- Which area of intimacy is it most difficult to freely open up yourself to? How do you want to show up differently in that area with your spouse?

HIS PERSPECTIVE

When tying the knot in our early 20s, Danielle and I were virgins who had a ton to learn about not only physical intimacy but also how our spiritual transparency held the key for the deep connection we now possess. We learned that if we were going to have a lasting connection, it was hinged on our ability to be honest with each other about our "intimacy killers." We found that these were the areas that carried the most shame because they were typically imperfections, weaknesses, and vulnerabilities. This is why it's essential not to be judgmental and critical with your spouse because it's knowing that you're admired and loved for who you are instead of who you are not – that allows intimacy in marriage to flourish.

HER PERSPECTIVE

Although Howard and I married as virgins, we both had baggage to deal with from our childhoods and histories from previous relationships to discuss and bring to the forefront, no matter how embarrassing and shameful it was. Thankfully, we decided to be transparent with each other early on, which helped me to build my trust and confidence in him from the onset. It allowed us to have open communication about our weaknesses and faults, leading to the creation of boundaries and checkpoints that have helped us to remain faithful all these years.

It has been vital for me in the area of intimacy to remember that my body is not my own and to act accordingly. I've talked to women whose husbands appear to be okay with no sex for extended periods of time for one reason or another, and I've talked to women whose men have taken every opportunity to shame and embarrass their wives for not making love to them. Both are flawed ways to approach physical intimacy. This approach can lead to bitterness and resentment harbored by both husband and wife. As a wife, it is important for us to keep the enemy at bay by valuing our husband's sexual and emotional needs, and having difficult conversations about any shaming that may be going on. In doing so, we can build a healthy line of communication around our sex life while doing our best to satisfy our husband sexually.

CASE STUDY

Jason and Fong were both previously married before they met each other and had kids. At the start of their marriage everything was great, and they were both satisfied with each other sexually. After a few years, however, their sex life was not living up to their expectations. Each afraid to discuss the issues, their sex life suffered and eventually became non-existent. An entire year passed and they had barely even kissed or held hands. When Jason finally brought up the fact that they hadn't slept together in nearly a year, Fong became very defensive and accused Jason of cheating. Appalled and offended, Jason responded angrily. He said the only reason he brought up the issue was that he saw her ex-husband in the grocery store. He recounted that of all the conversations and confessions they had about her ex, never did she complain about the intimacy in her previous marriage. Determined to get to the root of the issue, he asked her directly what was holding her back from making love to him. After a short while of avoiding the issue, Fong confessed that she no longer felt emotionally connected to Jason and therefore, felt like they were just roommates. She explained how she felt they had drifted apart, and the sparks that used to fly between them were long gone. Determined to seek help for their relationship, they entered counseling.

Discuss with your spouse (or group) the takeaways from this case study. How could Jason and Fong have prevented the drift that caused them to experience a sexual drought?

LIFE APPLICATION

With your spouse, take turns listening to one another as to what areas you each feel there is a deficit in your intimacy. Be gentle and non-accusatory as you do, using "I feel..." statements. Discuss how you both might help the other feel safe and how you can each take the next step of trust in your intimacy. Set up a plan with tangible steps that you can take as a couple to invest in your intimacy.

_____

_____

_____

> " Didn't the Lord make you one with your wife? In body and spirit you are his. And what does he want? Godly children from your union. So guard your heart; remain loyal to the wife of your youth. - Malachi 2:15

Reflections:

FINAL THOUGHTS

It is impossible to write an exhaustive workbook on marriage. Honestly, we could have written eight more chapters if we thought it would help. But rather than micromanaging your marriage, our prayer has always been to help you understand what it takes to truly work with each other and God towards a healthy marriage that thrives as you implement these fundamental principles. Your work is obviously not done. It is highly unlikely that you have "completed" your foundation in these last eight weeks. If nothing else, it will take time and repetition of these healthy habits for this foundation to set fully. Not to mention the unexpected cracks that all marriages form over time.

As you continue to build, hit roadblocks, and work through difficulties in your marriage, we hope that you will refer back to this workbook and find guidance in going back to the "basics" for lack of a better word. In our experience, so much pain can be avoided by reassessing your marriage and how well you are talking through and implementing these fundamentals of marriage. And perhaps if you have heard nothing else, understand that your marriage will only be as strong as your support team (friends, family, pastors, counselors, each other, and most of all God). Without these important relationships, we know we would not be as far along in our marital health.

We pray that God uses these Fundamentals of Marriage to help you and your spouse build the beautiful and powerful marriage that He has always intended for you. A marriage that towers to the sky, drawing others' eyes upward to the one who helped you get there, your Good Architect and Lord.

30-DAY PRAYER CHALLENGE

PRAYING TOGETHER

> **For where two or three have gathered together in My name, I am there in their midst. - Matthew 18:20**

Praying together (and for each other) consistently invites God in and gives Him the opportunity to do infinitely more than we can ever ask or think. Prayer is simply talking to God and having the faith that he listens and wants good things for us. We can talk to God aloud, alone, silently, or with others. No matter which way you choose, God is always waiting to hear from you and is the absolute best listener.

In marriage, something amazingly intimate and passionate happens when we pray with our husband or wife. We become open, humble, and vulnerable in the sight of our spouse, knowing that we are fully dependent on the grace and mercy of God to iron out the kinks in our character and relationships. Couples that pray together acknowledge that they and their marriage are not (and never will be) perfect and because of that fully depend on God. Only He can help us become the best version of a husband or wife we can be.

On the next page is a **30-Day Prayer Challenge** for you and your spouse. It is an opportunity for you to build a rhythm of prayer into your and marriage.

Over the next 30 days, pray for each other in the following areas:

To grow spiritually	To be able to balance priorities
That God would bless the work of your hands	To conquer every test and trial
That your marriage will be a positive influence on others	For favor, open doors, divine appointments, and opportunities
That you will strive to love and respect each other	To exhibit leadership
That you will exhibit healthy communication	To grow in character
That you are able to forgive when offended	That God would send accountability partners and mentors
That you will have boldness in witnessing to others	That your friendships will be edifying, positive, and uplifting
That you will have a healthy temperament and stable emotional health	That you will be each other's best friend
That your intimacy, passion, and romance stays fresh	To submit to one another without resentment
That you will be good money managers	To have good work ethic
To resist lust and temptation	To be encouraged
Against strongholds, addictions, or struggles	To move as one
That you will be in good health	To treat each other with grace
That your minds and spirits will be at peace	To be gentle and kind to each other
To identify and operate in your purpose, gifts, and callings	To be slow to speak, quick to listen, and slow to anger

Marriage Resources

Marriage on Deck - marriageondeck.com

Howard and Danielle Taylor, the Founders of Marriage on Deck, offer premarital coaching, marriage coaching, and marital readiness for singles. We would love to speak at your next Relationship Conference, Marriage Retreat, or Singles Event! For more information, visit our website or email us at:

hello@marriageondeck.com.

Follow us!

Facebook: Marriage on Deck

Instagram: Marriage on Deck

YouTube: Marriage on Deck

National Healthy Marriage Resource Center - healthymarriageinfo.org

Download free, cutting-edge resources published by the National Healthy Marriage Resource Center! The research section of their website includes documents that summarize and synthesize a vast body of recent marital statistics and research, list and describe many of the major sources of this data, and provide links to other documents and organizational resources to help you in your marriage.

American Association of Marriage and Family Therapy - aamft.org

The American Association for Marriage and Family Therapy (AAMFT) is the professional association for the field of marriage and family therapy. If you or someone you know is experiencing distress, therapy with a marriage and family therapist (MFT) can help. The AAMFT represents the professional interests of more than 50,000 marriage and family therapists throughout the United States, Canada, and abroad.

Made in the USA
Las Vegas, NV
19 January 2021

16176285R00059